Making It Better

A play

James Saunders

Samuel French - London
New York - Toronto - Hollywood

ISBN 0 573 01834 0

Please see page iv for further copyright information.

MAKING IT BETTER

First presented at the Hampstead Theatre, London, on
6th February 1992, with the following cast:

Diana Harrington	Jane Asher
Tomas Kratky	Rufus Sewell
Adrian Harrington	Larry Lamb
Josef Pavlicek	David De Keyser
Newsreader	Sylvester Morand

Directed by Michael Rudman
Lighting Design by Rory Dempster
Design by Simon Higlett
Time—Act I Scene 1 and Act II Scene 5—1992
   The rest of the play—1989

COPYRIGHT INFORMATION

(See also page ii)

CHARACTERS

Diana Harrington
Tomas Kratky
Adrian Harrington
Josef Pavlicek

SYNOPSIS OF SCENES

ACT I

ACT II

Other plays by James Saunders
Published by Samuel French Ltd

After Liverpool (with Games)
Barnstable
Bodies
Double Double
Games (with After Liverpool)
Mixed Doubles (with other authors)

ACT I

The café area of the departure lounge at London Airport. 1992

There is a general hum of airport noises

Diana sits at a table, hand luggage and duty-free bag at her feet, reading a newspaper

The departure of a flight to Prague is announced

Tomas enters, in a light business suit and an open topcoat, carrying an executive briefcase. He approaches Diana and looks at her for a few moments before speaking

Tomas Hallo, Diana.
Diana (*looking up sharply*) Oh my God.

They remain still for a moment, Diana staring, Tomas smiling

Tomas Such a surprise. I tried to find you. I telephoned to Bush House, but they said you don't work for World Service Radio now. (*He sits down at the table*)
Diana Why didn't you try the flat?
Tomas But I thought you moved.
Diana No, I'm still there.
Tomas Ah! I telephoned, nobody answered but I thought you moved anyway. And then I had to go to Birmingham, I was only here a week, a lot of business to do. What a pity. Next time perhaps. . . . You are going on holiday? Can I buy you a coffee or something else?
Diana I've got something coming. (*She gives a sudden quick glance away, towards the bar, then back to Tomas*)
Tomas Ah.
Diana What were you doing here?
Tomas I told you, business. I'm a business man now, you see. (*He indicates his clothing*)

Diana looks at him seriously

Tomas gives a little deprecatory laugh

Diana So you're not going to write books and become famous?
Tomas Aha. I remember that. I was a young man then.
Diana Three years ago.
Tomas Three years can be a long time. A lot of things have happened to me,

I'm a grown-up man now. I have a little boy, you know. Another Tomas.
He looks like me.

Diana And a wife?

Tomas Yes, a wife too.

There is a slight pause

Diana They've called your flight.

Tomas That's OK. (*He sits looking at her, smiling slightly*) So how are you,
what are you doing now?

Diana I'm in advertising; making commercials. I mean I work for a
company that makes commercials.

Tomas Good money?

Diana Yes, quite good money.

Tomas And you are happy?

Diana Oh yes. And you?

Tomas I'm busy. Whenever I'm busy I'm happy ... You are beautiful as
always.

Diana looks at him for a moment

Did I say something wrong?

Diana No. no.

Tomas Listen, you must come to Prague, see how it is now. I will show you
around. You can stay at our house. We have a big house.

Diana Thank you.

Tomas I think about you sometimes. You think about me sometimes?

Diana Yes, sometimes.

Tomas We had good times then.

Diana Yes.

He sits smiling at her

Black-out

SCENE 2

The living-room of Diana's flat in London. Evening. 1989

*There are three entrances into the room, one from the bedroom, one from the
kitchen and one from the rest of the flat. There is a curtained window, and a
sofa, dining table and chairs, drinks cabinet, CD player, radio and telephone
are in appropriate places*

*A pile of papers, typewritten sheets with handwritten annotations, lies on the
floor next to a chair*

Music is playing on the CD player

There is the sound of the front door opening

After a moment, Adrian enters, carrying a thick foolscap envelope. He looks toward the kitchen

Adrian Hallo?
Diana (*off*) Hallo.
Adrian Hubby's home!
Diana (*off*) Whoopee! You're late, where've you been?
Adrian In the club. You know what it's like ... (*He pours a drink*) I'm getting a drink, do you want one?
Diana (*off*) I'm having cocoa.
Adrian God what a day. And now I've got to read two bloody plays tonight. Script conference in the morning. You know the idiots forgot to clear copyright on that play by what's-his-name?

Diana enters, carrying a mug of cocoa. She heads for her chair

Adrian kisses Diana on the cheek as she passes

Diana Didn't you check?
Adrian It slipped my mind. What with one thing and another ... What are you doing?
Diana (*sitting*) Juggling programmes as usual. Then I'm taking my cocoa to bed.
Adrian Di ...
Diana Yes?
Adrian Listen, I've been chewing things over—
Diana Oh, have you had anything to eat? You know you're supposed to eat.
Adrian I had a roll in the club.
Diana You had a roll in the club?
Adrian Di, there's something I want to talk about. About our situation.
Diana I was just going to bed.
Adrian If you could give me a moment. (*He turns off the music*) The first thing I want to say is that I appreciate how you've coped with everything, I mean coped with a situation that could have been pretty bloody difficult. Don't think it hasn't been appreciated. I shall be eternally grateful ... The fact is, love, I've decided to more or less come out.
Diana (*after a slight pause*) More or less?
Adrian Well, you know. I mean I'm not about to announce it in *The Times*.
Diana I thought you'd more or less come out already. The whole of Bush House knows. All your friends know. Everyone knows except your mother. Are you going to tell your mother?
Adrian That's not my immediate concern—
Diana I thought that's what coming out meant, telling your mother.
Adrian Diana, I wish you'd let me explain myself ... It's not to do with who happens to know and who happens not to know, it's to do with—it's a question of—the way I present myself, my willingness to accept myself for what I am, which means to allow myself to be seen to be what I am in the public—
Diana Convenience?

Adrian Oh, for God's sake ... (*He goes to get himself another drink*)
Diana I'm sorry, Adrian. That was absolutely unforgivable. (*But she giggles*)
Adrian Diana, I happen to be serious.
Diana You want to move out.
Adrian What?
Diana Or are you wanting *me* to move out?
Adrian No no no no no, of course not. You stay here, Di, no question of that ... I should have done it ages ago. It's been bloody unfair on you ... (*He pauses*)
Diana Have you a date in mind?
Adrian I thought fairly soon. No point in stretching it out once the die's been cast. Don't you think?
Diana Have you got somewhere to go?
Adrian Yes, as it happens Phil Patten's off to America for a couple of months, did you know? He says I can use his place. Just while I'm looking. It'll be doing him a favour in fact. Feed the cat and so on. Keep the burglars away.
Diana When's he going?
Adrian End of the week. Of course I don't have to move in immediately.
Diana Only somebody's got to feed the cat.
Adrian I'm not doing it for the cat, love.
Diana It might have been a good idea if *we'd* talked about it.
Adrian That's what we're doing.
Diana As a *fait accompli.*
Adrian Not at all. Nothing's decided.
Diana Of course it's decided. If you want to go you'll go.
Adrian Di, I just want to do the right thing by both of us.
Diana And we can't disappoint the cat ... Sorry, it just seems a bit sudden. I don't know why, it's been on the cards long enough. Hasn't it?
Adrian It's not that I want to go. I mean it's been all right, hasn't it? I mean that's the ridiculous thing. We get on very well together, don't we?
Diana Yes, I suppose we do.
Adrian I think we've coped remarkably well. It says a lot for the relationship. It's just the bloody biological factor.

There is a pause

Diana Hm.
Adrian What?
Diana Yes. Yes, Adrian ... Twenty years. A good round number to finish on.
Adrian That's one way of looking at it.
Diana Good, right. I'm taking my cocoa to bed. You'd better read those scripts, if you can still focus. We don't want the World Service to grind to a halt, do we? (*She gets up*)
Adrian Diana ...
Diana Yes?
Adrian You're all right?

Diana Yes. Of course. Top hole. Don't worry. Good night. (*She moves to leave. As she passes Adrian, she puts her hand briefly on his head*)

Adrian raises his hand to touch Diana, but is too late as:

Diana exits

Black-out

SCENE 3

The same. Late afternoon

Pavlicek's hat rests on a chair

Pavlicek is standing in the doorway to the bedroom, partly dressed, tying his tie

Diana, dressing-gowned, comes in from the kitchen with a tray on which is a coffee-pot, cups and saucers, milk jug and sugar bowl. Diana puts the tray down, pours herself a cup of black coffee and takes a sip. She is still for a moment

Pavlicek watches her

There is the sound of a police car passing the window. As the sound dies away:

Diana goes to the window and looks out

Pavlicek Is he there?
Diana Who?
Pavlicek Isn't it a Graham Greene novel? The last refuge of the ageing spy. There should be a man on the corner in a raincoat.
Diana Help yourself to coffee.
Pavlicek Let me guess: if I had been English, it would have been Nescaf?
Diana I don't make a habit of picking up strangers.
Pavlicek But we met once. Some BBC reception or other. We talked about the Bohemian countryside. You remember?
Diana I'm afraid not.
Pavlicek You wore something blue-grey and drank orange juice.
Diana Anyway, I don't usually go shopping for men at lunchtime. Just to make it clear.
Pavlicek Something pleasant happened, I'm happy to leave it there ...

Diana crosses to the telephone and dials

Yes, Bush House will be wondering what has happened to you. Perhaps they'll put the police on the case. The man on the corner, is he one of theirs, do you think?
Diana You read a lot of spy novels?
Pavlicek Oh yes.
Diana (*into the phone*) ... two-zero-one please.... Sue—Diana. Terribly

sorry, I suddenly came over all unnecessary and went home. I tried to ring you but you were engaged. . . . No, I went to bed for a while. . . . Yes, I've taken something, I feel much better now. . . . What? . . . No no! Tell Felix we can't possibly re-programme, it'll upset the whole schedule. . . . Thanks, love. See you in the morning then. . . . Yes, I'm fine, really, 'bye. (*She puts the phone down*)

Pavlicek So I class as medicinal? Perhaps I should set up a clinic, do I see a market opportunity—?

Diana You don't have to make conversation, for God's sake.

Pavlicek I beg your pardon.

There is a pause

Would you like me to go now?

Diana looks across at him for a moment before she answers

Diana Sit down and drink your coffee.

Pavlicek sits obediently

There is another pause

Pavlicek When I arrived in this country, you know, I had very little English. But I was so besotted with the idea of free speech that I talked constantly, whether I made sense or not. And I'm afraid the habit has persisted.

Diana When did you come here?

Pavlicek Oh, a long time ago.

Diana *I* knew Prague once; also a long time ago.

Pavlicek But it still excites me, English freedom. Talking without looking over the shoulder first. Actually choosing one's politicians! And still amazes me how you all take it for granted.

Diana Do we?

Pavlicek Don't you remember in the pub, grumbling about your government as if it's a kind of bad weather? As if it had been wished on you?

Diana It was, on me. I didn't vote for this lot.

Pavlicek But then it can be wished off again, can't it? Two, three years' time.

Diana You think I should be dancing in the street, then?

Pavlicek They would in Prague . . . Democracy shows people a picture of themselves; they can change it if they wish. What other truth do you want, but to see yourselves as you are? Perhaps your discontent is a purely personal affair, to do with yourself only. History takes care of itself, we worry too much about it. You think?

Diana Well, I'm sorry I bleated on about it.

Pavlicek No, please . . . (*He pauses, looks at his watch, puts down his cup and stands up*) So . . .

Diana You don't have to go yet. I'm not expecting another client.

Pavlicek To tell the truth, I'm swimming in unfamiliar waters.

Diana It's like going to the pictures in the afternoon, isn't it? No dark to hide in when you come out.

Pavlicek Why do you want to hide?

Diana (*getting up*) I'm going to have a Scotch, if you want one.

Pavlicek No thank you. I've already had more than was good for me.

Diana I didn't notice.

Pavlicek I surprised myself.

Diana (*pouring herself a Scotch*) You said in the pub you're a journalist . . .

Pavlicek I *was* a journalist. I still do a little piece now and then, where I can, the Czech view, that kind of thing.

Diana What else?

Pavlicek Oh, I give Czech lessons, not a booming industry. The odd translation for the World Service . . .

Diana You can't live on what we give you.

Pavlicek Oh, my spying, I forgot that.

Diana What?

Pavlicek A joke. No, one lives quite well, with care. And to tell you a secret, I have a contact in Bush House, which gives me fairly open access.

Diana To what?

Pavlicek To the canteen. The food is very cheap and quite good. London is a cornucopia if one knows where to look . . .

Diana gets up to pour herself another drink

Do you drink rather a lot?

She stares at him

It's none of my business.

Diana No it isn't.

Pavlicek May I join you after all?

Diana pours him a whisky

One tends to think of oneself as the main character in a long important novel. This is a great mistake. Much better to bè a peripheral character in a book of short stories, don't you think?

Diana Hm . . . (*She gives him his drink and sits down*)

There is a pause

Pavlicek Do you want to tell me about yourself?

Diana gives him a long stare

A silence

Diana God, I'm a fool. Dubsky. That gossip. Of course I've seen you with him.

Pavlicek I'm sorry?

Diana So *he*'s the one who signs you in. He tells you all the news, does he? Goings-on in Bush House? (*She pauses slightly*) Hm?

Pavlicek Your husband no longer lives with you. Yes, he mentioned it. Again it's none of my business.

Diana Then perhaps you can stop pontificating; I expect it's an occupational hazard of middle-aged refugees, is it, playing being wise in funny accents?

Pavlicek I'm sorry if I—

Diana No, I'm not really bothered about the government, it's just a woman's emotional problems.

Pavlicek I was not quite saying that . . .

Diana And then, hot with the gossip, who should you see in the *Wellington* looking, what was it?—*disgruntled* but the lady herself; what a chance to play your part and see what comes of it. Oh yes, London is a cornucopia. And now you can go home and write a short story about it. Read it to all your friends. (*She drinks*)

Pavlicek We had an encounter in a pub, which finished in a bedroom. Your husband has left. Yes, it might stretch to a short story.

There is a slight pause

Diana Yes, all right . . . And why should I blame you? It was my idea.

Pavlicek Oh dear, and I thought it was mine. But I see no necessity for blame in either direction. Nor, may I add, for regret, at least on my side.

Diana (*with a little laugh*) Well that's cleared that up. (*She pauses*) We parted on amicable terms. Pass it on . . . I daresay you're right: discontent is one's own business.

Pavlicek More precisely, the emotional component of one's discontent. It's possible to be unhappy and yet glad for the world; or happy while wishing for better things around one.

Diana I mean I wasn't too bothered about the government half an hour ago.

Pavlicek And I'd quite forgotten my motherland. Sleep and sex are great comforts.

Diana And spy novels?

Pavlicek Yes . . . So . . . (*He looks at his watch*) Oh good Lord . . . (*He gets up*)

Diana Do you want to go back into the bedroom? See it round again as they say?

Pavlicek Ah.

Diana You don't.

Pavlicek I am not quite as young as I used to be . . .

Diana We can give it a whirl, can't we?

Pavlicek (*hesitating*) Yes . . . yes, yes . . .

Diana Oh, forget it.

Pavlicek I'm sorry, I shouldn't really be here.

Diana I know that.

Pavlicek I mean I should be elsewhere . . . To tell the truth I should be finding myself a room. A bedsit, you know. I had a very pleasant bedsit in Finsbury Park. But, alas, they find they can make more money if they turn the house into flats and sell the flats. So I have to find somewhere else.

Diana Is it urgent?

Pavlicek Fairly urgent.

Diana By when?

Pavlicek By today actually.

Diana You mean for tomorrow?

Pavlicek No, I mean for today. I meant to spend this afternoon looking, but something came up as you know.

Diana Oh God.

Pavlicek So I really should go, you see.

Diana Do you mean you've nowhere to stay?

Pavlicek Not at the moment, no.

Diana They must have given you notice.

Pavlicek Oh yes, the statutory week. Only—

Diana When?

Pavlicek A week ago.

Diana So what have you been doing since?

Pavlicek Oh I looked at some places, but they were not salubrious. I am writing a play, you know, I think it will be very good. I hope they will do it on the World Service. I wanted to speak to your—Adrian Harrington about it this morning, but he was not available. They should do more political plays, don't you think so?

Diana So where are you going to sleep?

Pavlicek I'm sure something will turn up.

Diana A cardboard box?

Pavlicek I can stay in a hotel for the night.

Diana Where's your luggage?

Pavlicek I left a case in Bush House. It will be quite safe there.

Diana They'll think it's a bomb.

Pavlicek No no, there's a typewriter with it.

Diana So you're going to wander the streets in the rain with your case and your typewriter looking for some sleazy hotel.

Pavlicek Is it raining? Oh, very Graham Greene. No, the Strand Palace is close.

Diana The Strand Palace! . . . Have you any money?

Pavlicek I should pay you? Forgive me, it was another joke. Of course I have money. Do I look as if I don't have money?

Diana If you haven't enough for a hotel I can lend you some. That's all I'm saying.

Pavlicek Thank you, but I don't borrow money.

Diana Why not?

Pavlicek Because I forget to pay it back. Borrowed money makes bad blood.

Diana What's that, a Czech proverb? I'll remind you.

Pavlicek And then I don't have it and when I have it I forget again, no, I insist, thank you.

Diana Hotels are expensive. How much have you got?

Pavlicek This is extraordinary. (*He puts his hand in his pocket and brings out some coins*) Small change. Cheque book . . . (*He brings out a cheque book, then a pocket book*) And here, you see, notes. You have seen that I wear underwear, you noticed a small hole in the vest but I was not prepared for the occasion. This is a handkerchief, you see. Fountain pen. They also owe me money at Bush House. Do I pass muster?

Diana Well, if this is the way you like to do things.

Pavlicek Yes. My funny foreign way.

Diana You'd better go and rescue your case before they blow it up.

Pavlicek Yes. Thank you so much, it was extremely pleasant. I'm sorry I can't stay. (*He goes up to Diana, takes her hand and kisses her gently*) I should like to discuss my play with you. If I ring your office some time we can have a cup of coffee perhaps?

Diana Drama is not really my department—

Pavlicek No no, to discuss the ideas only. I have Czech friends, of course, but I would appreciate the views of an English person with a knowledge of the background and so on. Well, we shall see . . . Au revoir; and thank you.

Diana Your hat.

Pavlicek Oh yes. (*He picks it up and moves to the door as Diana speaks*)

Diana (*looking out at the rain*) Are you allowed to borrow an umbrella, or is there a Czech proverb?

Pavlicek I'm sorry, I don't think I can cope with the typewriter and the case and the umbrella.

Diana Then leave it!

Pavlicek Yes . . . Well, goodbye, Diana.

Diana Goodbye—

Pavlicek Josef.

Diana Josef.

Pavlicek Of course what I could do . . .

Diana What?

Pavlicek Only I don't want to bother you.

Diana You've bothered me already. I shall be bothered all the evening wondering how you got on.

Pavlicek In that case what I could do is perhaps use your telephone to find somewhere? They can be rather funny at Bush House.

Diana (*after a slight pause*) Yes, you could do that.

Pavlicek I'll pay for the calls.

Diana Don't be ridiculous.

Pavlicek Shall I do that then?

Diana Yes, why not?

Pavlicek Good.

Black-out

SCENE 4

The same. Morning

On the floor by the door are the components of a word processor and several cardboard boxes

Tomas is wandering idly about the room, looking and touching; he might be trying to commit the room to memory

Diana comes in with a black stiff-covered exercise book in her hands. She goes to the phone and dials

Diana (*into the phone*) It's Diana. I can't find any blue book. Only a black book ... About ten by—eight ... OK ... Yes? Bell's. I'll tell him ... Yes ... *Yes*. How's the leg? ... Hard luck ... Yes, I'll tell him. Do you want to talk to him? ... All right, I'll ... Yes. 'Bye. (*She puts the phone down*) This is the one. (*She puts the book down*) Oh, he wants you to get a bottle of Bells on the way.
Tomas A bottle of Bells?
Diana Whisky. Bell's whisky.
Tomas Please, how much is Bell's whisky?
Diana I don't know. A tenner will cover it. Ten pounds.
Tomas I don't have ten pounds. Maybe you have ten pounds?

Diana hesitates, then takes a ten pound note from her bag and gives it to him

Diana What country are you from?
Tomas I am Czech. From Prague.
Diana Another one?
Tomas I'm sorry?
Diana How did they let you out?
Tomas They allowed me to come to London for my studies.
Diana Isn't that unusual?
Tomas Well, I am here.
Diana Yes. (*She pauses*) Well, give Adrian my regards.
Tomas I will do that. (*He picks up the book and moves towards the word processor. He stops*) I wonder, could I please have a glass of water?
Diana Water?
Tomas Please.

Diana exits into the kitchen

Tomas puts the book down again

There is a pause

Diana enters with a glass of water

Diana There you are.
Tomas Thank you. (*He takes a sip*)

There is a pause

Diana looks steadily at Tomas

Diana Young young young man ...
Tomas Yes I am young.

There is a slight pause

Diana Is he in pain? Adrian?
Tomas His leg? Yes, I think so, when he moves.
Diana He'd better stay still then, hadn't he?

There is a slight pause

Diana *Co studujete v Londýně?*
Tomas Ah, you speak Czech!
Diana Yes, I—
Tomas You have a good accent. Better than my English one, I think. Only here I speak only English.

Diana says nothing

To answer your question, I study biochemistry. I do post-graduate research on moulds.
Diana On what?
Tomas Moulds. Like on bad food.
Diana I see.
Tomas How interesting.
Diana Sorry?
Tomas People say "How interesting" when they don't know something else to say.
Diana (*bridling*) No well, I confess it's not a topic I'm terribly *au fait* with. The two-culture syndrome, C. P. Snow and all that, you know?
Tomas I expect you just want to talk politics. Everyone talks about politics just now.
Diana Is there something wrong with that?
Tomas No no . . .
Diana Or aren't you concerned with what's going on at the moment? Do you think you're too young to be bothered with it?
Tomas No please, I don't say against talking politics. And I do know what happens in Poland and Soviet Union and so. But I have other things I want to be interested in.
Diana Moulds.
Tomas Yes, I study moulds for my paper I must write. But then I study the origin of life, how it comes out of non-life, how it develops, how an organism change to stay alive and so. I have many ideas. In some years I think I will come famous.
Diana Well bravo . . . So you're working out where we've all come from.
Tomas Yes, you can say I want to do that. Because, you see—
Diana And when you've done that will you be able to tell us where we're going?

There is a slight pause

Tomas Where we are going is to die; and then the species to change and then to die. And then the world to die. That is not my interest. You must ask a priest, I think. (*He pauses*) You don't want to ask me if I like to be in England?

Diana No. Should I?

Tomas (*smiling*) Everybody else does. What they mean is, how terrible to live in Czechoslovakia!

Diana Well? Is it?

Tomas Like the bird say to the fish, "How terrible to live in the water!"

Diana So you like it there.

Tomas It's my place. I learn to swim there.

Diana And now you're here—

Tomas Now I'm here I learn to swim here. It's OK.

Diana So you're saying there's no difference. Whatever the country, whatever the conditions, whatever the restrictions—

Tomas No no. Please. Of course there's difference. A lot of people in Czechoslovakia want things to change, they want it like it is in the West. But I still got to live there so I make it the best.

Diana Make the best of it.

Tomas I mean I learn to swim well. What else should I do?

Diana Try and *change* things?

Tomas Yes, some want to do that. Is their way of swimming. I hope they succeed if this is what you ask, I can say that here; but for me like I said I have other things I want to do, important things . . . (*He pauses slightly*) You look at me as if I said something wrong. Is the same anywhere. Don't you do what you want to do? Is a lot of people in England do what they don't want to do? Maybe that's true. They look like it.

Diana What do you mean?

Tomas I mean people here don't seem very content or happy. Free country or not free country. Is a pity. Like you perhaps.

Diana What like me?

Tomas *You* are not content, I think.

Diana How content I am, young man, is my own business. And how content are you?

Tomas I'm partly content, thank you.

Diana Only partly?

Tomas Yes, only partly. Some things I want and try to get. But I'm OK. I like what I do, I like my life.

Diana Well bully for you. How are you taking the stuff? Do you want a taxi?

Tomas No, I have a car, Adrian's car.

Diana Where?

Tomas Out there.

Diana (*looking out of the window*) You're on a double yellow. They could clamp it.

Tomas Adrian said it doesn't matter because it's Saturday.

Diana Adrian is wrong. (*She turns to the window for a moment, then back*) How long have you known him?

Tomas Not long. Some weeks.

Diana Some *weeks*?

Tomas Yes, some weeks.
Diana How did you meet him? In a bar somewhere?
Tomas In your World Service radio building. Bush House.
Diana What were you doing there?
Tomas I was in the canteen. Your Josef made it so that I could use the canteen.
Diana Who?
Tomas Josef Pavlicek who stays here.
Diana You know Josef?
Tomas He is old friend of my father. He's my godfather actually, for what that means. I only just now heard he lives here, I didn't see him since some time.
Diana He hasn't mentioned you. Do you go to those meetings of his?
Tomas His Wednesdays with his old men? I went to some at first, now I keep away. But I'm glad he's here. His room where he lived, it was a— *brloh*?
Diana Hovel.
Tomas A hovel. He did his cooking on a gas on the table. Twenty-one years in this country and he lives in a room with a gas on the table. But this is OK. He must be comfortable here.
Diana It's just till he finds somewhere else. And where are *you* staying?
Tomas (*surprised*) You mean in London? With Adrian now, of course.
Diana Ah.
Tomas I was already looking for a room, you see.
Diana And you happened to get talking to Adrian ...
Tomas Yes yes, in the canteen in Bush House and he said I could stay with him. So—I am there.
Diana That was kind of him.
Tomas I think you know what is kind. (*He looks at her steadily for a moment*)

She stares back

Diana What?
Tomas Sorry, my English is not very good now, yet, I understand more than I can say. It will get better. Soon I will speak very good English. Thank you for the water. My name is Tomas. Tomas Kratky. I will see you again. Perhaps I will bring you a book on how life started, there is a very good one.
Diana Please don't bother—
Tomas Yes, I will do that. It will change how you see the world, then you will feel better.
Diana You'd better go now.
Tomas Yes. And when you have read the book perhaps we can—
Diana There's a warden down there.

Black-out

SCENE 5

The South Bank of the Thames, outside the National Film Theatre. Late evening. Summer

A public bench stands facing the river

Diana and Pavlicek, who carries a hat, approach from the Festival Hall

Pavlicek The story goes that some foreigner or other once lived for months or years in Bush House, and nobody knew. He washed in the lavatories and ate in the canteen and slept in an office, or a cupboard. Everybody assumed he had a right to be there because he was foreign.

Diana Was it you?

Pavlicek (*laughing*) No no ... (*Indicating the bench*) This is where the bag lady ate her strawberries.

Diana What? (*She sits*)

Pavlicek (*sitting*) Some weeks ago there was a small awards ceremony at the National Film Theatre followed by a buffet supper. The evening was warm so the doors to the riverside were open, people wandered outside with their food ... So I wandered in. There was a bag lady sitting here watching the goings-on; so I took two of everything, two chicken legs, two slices of beef, two of ham, and so on; a number of paper napkins. She wrapped her pieces carefully and stowed them in one of her bags. She said nothing so I respected her silence. Around us they chatted of films and art and politics, we sat silently in that beautiful evening, I eating, she not, gazing across the river to where the light in the tower assured us that Parliament was still in session ...

Diana London as cornucopia.

Pavlicek I went in for another glass of wine. When I came out she was eating strawberries and cream.

Diana No handouts going tonight.

Pavlicek Oh yes! A free view! ... You enjoyed the concert.

Diana You shouldn't have paid so much for the tickets.

Pavlicek What's money, my dear?

Diana It's that stuff you never have any of.

Pavlicek Didn't I tell you? Bush House laid me a golden egg last week; a little one, a plover's egg.

Diana Which you spend on concert tickets when you've got holes in the soles of your shoes.

Pavlicek Not all of it; a plover's egg, not a quail's egg ... If God had wanted me to worry about holes in my shoes He'd not have invented cardboard.

They laugh. There is a pause

Martinů was born in a belfry, you know. His parents lived in a tower. He could see the whole town from his window, and the Moravian countryside beyond. You can hear it in his music.

Diana You still miss your country.

Pavlicek Yes of course.

Diana Things are changing. Who knows who'll be next? Perhaps you should have stayed; seen it out.

Pavlicek I had a friend, you know, an old friend, a school chum. Also a journalist. When the Hungarian uprising was put down I thought quite seriously of suicide; the other way of escape. Easier really, no visa, no barbed wire. But he talked me out of it. Then in sixty-eight I tried to persuade him to come over with me and he tried to talk me out of that too. But this time he was not successful, though his arguments were the same.

Diana What were they?

Pavlicek That I was running away. That I had a duty to work from within. That everything changes, nothing is permanent, the history of middle Europe is a history of sitting tight and waiting for things to go away. We argued a long time, to tell the truth we had a terrible row. He called me a coward. Then he stayed and I went. That's all. Also he had a wife and child, you see, and I had a wife only.

Diana Only ... (*She pauses slightly*) And did he? Has he? Worked from within?

Pavlicek He is now the editor of his newspaper ...

Diana (*after a slight pause*) So you left your wife, just like that.

Pavlicek No, not just like that! I know it was a betrayal. I'm rather old-fashioned, as you've probably gathered.

Diana About marriage?

Pavlicek About promises. If you live with someone for a number of years there is an implicit promise; if not of fidelity, at least of continuity.

Diana An assumption; hardly a promise.

Pavlicek It is also in the vows.

Diana Who takes them seriously?

Pavlicek I do. They are vows. I betrayed her ... As Adrian betrayed you.

Diana Nonsense. You *are* old-fashioned. We happened to meet, we happened to get married, now we happen to be apart. That's all.

Pavlicek Is that what you said to each other? Shall we happen to marry? ... Where did you meet? Bush House?

Diana Prague in sixty-eight, believe it or not.

Pavlicek Really?

Diana Yes. Really. I'd taken my finals and went back there to celebrate. They were celebrating too, of course, we celebrated together ... Then one night the tanks rumbled in, and the next day I met Adrian, who was with a news team, and we came back and left them to it.

Pavlicek (*after a slight pause*) You've no children?

Diana No. I can't ... They'll get *this*, won't they? They wanted their freedom, they'll get it. No more socialist nonsense, conservatism for ever. Why not? It's what *we* want. (*She pauses*) Are you British now?

Pavlicek No, I remain Czech.

Diana So you still can't vote ... Was it worth it?

Pavlicek Was what worth what?

Diana Coming to live amongst us—dying ducks. Did you make an awful mistake? Were you betrayed too? Be honest.

Pavlicek My dear, I lived forty years in a country where my mind had to be a secret society; I know why I left. And I know what I lost. I agree, I get tired of that particular kind of Englishness, that grumbling that takes so little energy and so little thought and leaves everything as it was. I put up with it. I'm a well-mannered guest, I let you grumble and listen politely.

There is a pause

Diana This old friend of yours; is he Tomas's father?
Pavlicek Yes, of course. He'd have been about three when I left.
Diana You've kept him very dark.
Pavlicek I haven't seen much of him. He looked me up when he arrived, of course, I gave him tea in my little bedsit, I introduced him to various people—
Diana And to the canteen.
Pavlicek Through Dubsky, yes. The room he'd found for himself had no cooking facilities. Quite a slum in fact. It was clever of him to find Adrian and—accommodate himself. I'm sure he's much more comfortable now . . .
Diana Are you saying what I think you're saying?
Pavlicek Hm?
Diana You make him sound like a rent boy.
Pavlicek I wouldn't put it quite like that.
Diana It's what you're suggesting. That he's—with Adrian for what he can get. That's awful thing to say.
Pavlicek I'm sorry. I'm sure he's thoroughly homosexual.

There is a pause

Diana Thank you for taking me out.
Pavlicek My pleasure. (*He pauses*) I've been looking forward to this. I mean finishing my play and then taking you out somewhere to celebrate and then . . . I should very much like to make love to you again. (*He pauses*) I've made a mistake.
Diana I haven't said anything.

Pavlicek waits

   Josef, I don't want—
Pavlicek It's all right, it was only—
Diana I haven't finished! . . . I'm afraid it might turn into a kind of habitual thing and I've had enough of habitual things. That's all. Thank you for asking.
Pavlicek No no. I understand. I am most grateful to you, you know. (*He pauses slightly*) And I am looking for another place.
Diana Josef, you can't see the Houses of Parliament from here.
Pavlicek Who said you could?
Diana You did. You said you and your bag lady looked across—
Pavlicek Well then, it must have been somewhere else.
Diana It's getting chilly. (*She stands up*)

Pavlicek gets up too

Diana What do you do with your friends every Wednesday? Hatch plots?
Pavlicek We talk. Talk talk talk. The East is crumbling, great things are happening, we must talk about it, talk talk talk.
Diana Your hat.

Pavlicek picks up his hat and puts it on. Diana stands looking at him for a moment

Yes, all right, Josef.
Pavlicek All right what?
Diana Yes. Of course I will. What you asked. I'd love to. Thank you. Come on then. Let's celebrate.

Black-out

SCENE 6

The Club Room at Bush House. 1989

There is a table with two chairs

Adrian and Diana enter. Adrian walks with two sticks and carries a briefcase under his arm. Diana carries a tray with two cups of tea on it

Adrian Look, Di, try and see it from my point of view: we bought the flat when prices were low and now you're sitting on a lot of money.
Diana So what are you saying, you want me to move out so you can sell it?
Adrian I'm not suggesting that—
Diana I like it there, I don't want to move.
Adrian I'm not about to put you on the streets, love. Just listen to me. All I want is to get things on a legal footing.

Diana puts down the cups of tea, takes the briefcase from under Adrian's arm and arranges a chair for him. Adrian puts his sticks down and sits

Diana How long are you going to be on sticks?
Adrian A week or two. Bloody stupid thing to do. I should have warmed up first, I hadn't played squash for months.
Diana What were you doing, trying to prove something?
Adrian Could I have my briefcase?

Diana passes the briefcase to Adrian

(*Opening the briefcase and taking out papers*) You can keep all this stuff, I've got copies. Now, I had a word with an estate agent, and that's what he thinks we could get for the flat, here's his ... Then I got my accountant, here you are, to add it all up and take away the number he first thought of, and there's a figure at the bottom, you see, for what he thinks I'm due, what he calls a fair figure. Now ...
Diana Twenty thousand quid? I owe you twenty thousand quid?
Adrian Strictly speaking, yes. But what I propose is fifty percent of that. Say

the round ten thousand. (*He takes more papers from his case*) I asked the solicitor, to get it absolutely on a firm footing. Here's a copy of his letter. You can keep that.

Diana Why are you only asking for half what you think you're entitled to?

Adrian Look, Di, I feel rather embarrassed about all this . . .

Diana It's a high price to pay for a bit of embarrassment; ten thousand nicker. Anyway I haven't got it so you can't have it.

Adrian Di, please, don't jump to conclusions. I'm not asking for it now. It's a matter of getting it on paper. We just have to sign that agreement; you see, then if and when you pay me the money I sign another bit of bumf which gives you sole ownership, otherwise things stay as they are. It's a bloody good deal actually, from your point of view. Anyway I'll leave it all with you, think it over, no hurry. (*He picks up his tea and drinks*)

Diana looks at the papers

Oh Lord, I think Dubsky's coming over. Don't catch his eye.

Diana It's all right. He's decided we're having a post-marital discussion.

Adrian How are you, Di?

Diana Never been better. How are you? Oh, congratulations on your young man. He's very pretty. Rather arrogant, or do I mean pert? So *that's* why you wanted to leave.

Adrian I told you why I wanted to leave—

Diana You didn't tell me you had a young man lined up.

Adrian I wish you'd stop calling him a young man. And if you could keep your voice down a decibel or two . . .

Diana By the way, you owe me a tenner.

Adrian So I do. (*He gives her a note*)

Diana That's all I miss you for, I've got no one to be bitchy to. I love the way it rolls off you like water off a duck's back. Not even a real duck; a plastic one that goes in the bath. Push it under and up it pops. That's what first attracted me to you, your insensitivity, only I thought it was maturity . . . My romantic darling.

Adrian Have you been drinking?

Diana Don't you remember, all those years ago in Prague, calling me a romantic darling?

Adrian No.

Diana And I took your word for it. *You* didn't cry when the tanks came in.

Adrian I was very affected by it as a matter of fact.

Diana You weren't. It was just another job. Then you made it better. You were wise and calm and I stopped crying and came to your bed and you made it better. And hand in hand we skedaddled back to safe old England.

Adrian Diana . . .

Diana You were quite wrong. I wasn't in the least romantic. When they trundled in and took my city away I wanted to kill them, that's why I cried.

Adrian Diana, that was a hell of a long time ago.

Diana Yes it was. When Tiananmen Square happened I didn't cry, did I? I just thought, fuck it. Fuck them. Fuck them all . . . You've heard I've got *my*self a lodger too?

Adrian No. Already?

Diana Like you have already. Do you mean he hasn't told you about him?

Adrian Who?

Diana Your Tomas. They know each other. Mine is Czech too. We're suddenly infested with impecunious Czechs. You may have seen him in the canteen, Dubsky signs him in. Like your Tomas. So he'll be visiting. Isn't it cosy?

Adrian He hasn't mentioned a word of this to me. How did you get him?

Diana Picked him up in a bar. I was feeling a bit low in the *Wellington* one lunchtime, just after you left actually, and this codger came in and I thought: He'll do. I'll have him. So I brought him back. And it turned out he had nowhere to hang his hat—he wears a hat, he's an older man, you know I'm a pushover for older men—so I let him hang it at my place.

Adrian Well, it'll help with the mortgage repayments.

Diana Oh he hasn't got any money.

Adrian He's surely contributing?

Diana I let him pay half the electricity, to keep him quiet. Which means I go around switching off lights to save him money.

Adrian Is he staying for good?

Diana For good or ill.

Adrian I mean is it permanent?

Diana Nothing's permanent, Adrian, my love, you know that.

Adrian And erm . . .

Diana Yes. Whenever the mood takes me, I pad into his room and he obliges me. After all, I've got a washing machine, why shouldn't I have a . . . ? I tell you what, why don't you bring your lodger over one evening to meet my lodger and we'll do a swap on the carpet?

Adrian Oh really!

Diana Are you taking him with you?

Adrian Where?

Diana When you move. You haven't got long now, have you? Is the young man going with you? I mean Tomas. Is Tomas going with you?

Adrian I hope so.

Diana And what about Tomas? Does he hope so?

Adrian I really don't know.

Diana Isn't he returning your affections?

Adrian Di, you're getting a bit near the knuckle.

Diana Maybe I'll ask *him*. I'll have him round to tea, we can discuss you.

There is a slight pause

I need a holiday from this place. Do you ever wonder what we're doing here, Adrian? Not the news people, us British culture lot. Apart from teaching the foreigners English?

Adrian We do our jobs, Di . . .

Diana There's a revolution going on over there, and we give them culture and current affairs. What do we know that could possibly interest them now? We haven't been invaded, we haven't been occupied, we don't have to define what it means to be a country, we've got the *English* Channel to do that for us. We just sit cosy and safe on our bit of island, snug and smug and British, and think we know it all.

Adrian We do what we can, Diana. Culture matters. What do you think we should give them, agitprop? (*He pauses slightly*) I'm worried about you, Di.

Diana Why?

Adrian I wasn't just the lodger, you know. We've had a long relationship. There's an emotional price to be paid, I think you ought to be prepared—

Diana What *are* you talking about?

Adrian I'm talking about letting it out, Di, letting it go. Look, I didn't just want to see you to talk about the flat, I thought it might be helpful to you, and to me, if we—

Diana You're worried about playing your part properly, aren't you? Having heroically come out, though you still haven't told your mother I'll bet, now you want to play the understanding game. You want me to cry on your shoulder so you can make it better. Only you don't understand a fucking thing about me, you never did!

Adrian Di, I put up with a lot from you over the years. I don't have to any more. You're a free agent. If there's something you don't like, do something about it, if there's something you want, get it. Just stop bellyaching, will you?

Diana (*after a short pause*) Listen, I've got terribly randy since you left, I don't know why. Josef's out tonight, come back to my place and we'll go to bed for old times' sake. I've got a new trick.

Adrian I didn't mean that!

Diana Bugger tea, let's have a real drink. Scotch? My treat. (*She gets up and heads for the bar, ruffling Adrian's hair on her way past*)

Black-out

SCENE 7

Diana's flat. Early the same evening

The front door is heard to close

Diana enters, carrying a bag and the papers Adrian gave her. She throws her coat and bag down, opens the papers and glances at them. Throwing the papers down, she switches on the radio

A World Service news report is heard

Diana listens for a moment, then takes a new compact disc out of her bag and puts it in the player. She switches the radio off and the music on; it is the Suite from Strauss's "Der Rosenkavalier"

She exits into the kitchen

The doorbell rings

Diana comes out of the kitchen and exits through the door to the front door

She returns with Tomas. He is wearing new clothes and carrying a book

Diana If you've called to see Josef he's out.

Tomas With his old men, yes, I know that. It's OK, I came to see you. I was sitting a long time outside that pub on the corner of the street where I could watch when you come home.

Diana You might have sat there all night. I'd gone to see Adrian.

Tomas Yes I know that too. You had to talk about the flat. But I know he is going to the theatre tonight so I thought you would not be too long.

Diana Did he know you were coming here?

Tomas No, I don't have to tell him everything. You can tell him if you want to.

Diana Tomas, I find you a very confusing young man.

Tomas My English?

Diana No, not your English ... You can't stay long. I've got to get myself something to eat. Do you want a glass of water before you go?

Tomas Please, could I have perhaps a whisky instead, like you drink? To celebrate.

Diana Celebrate what?

Tomas Shall I say my new clothes? Adrian bought them for me. I said no but he said it gave him pleasure. You like them?

Diana Very fetching.

Tomas Fetching?

Diana (*pouring a whisky*) Do you want water with it?

Tomas No no. Like you have it.

Diana Did it get a ticket? ... The car.

Tomas A ticket. Yes, thank you.

Diana brings Tomas's drink over to him

Thank you. Cheers.

Diana switches off the CD player and sits

I think perhaps you are on the tall horse again.

Diana High horse.

Tomas High on a horse. I must be careful.

Diana I probably won't eat you. Sit down then.

Tomas I stand for a little while, do you mind?

Diana Afraid of creasing your new clothes?

Tomas No, I feel with energy, energetic. I play truant today, from work. Ah, here is the book I said I would bring. (*He gives her the book*) I wrote something inside, I hope that's OK.

Diana Did you buy this for me?

Tomas It's OK, Adrian gave me money for it. You are to read it right through, it will show you what a marvellous creature you are and how it came to be like that, no God, no magic, no miracle, all very simple. (*He wanders about the room, looking at things*)

Diana looks inside the book

C. P. Snow wrote books, I looked him up. He thought it's not good people don't know about thermodynamics. So now I see what you meant. You want me to explain you thermodynamics?

Diana I'll stay ignorant if you don't mind.

Tomas I get a feeling you don't think much about the work I do.

Diana Moulds?

Tomas No, what you came from, how you got here, why you are different from other things, that doesn't interest you?

Diana Why should it? I'm here and that's that. There's nothing I can do about it, is there? Or you either.

Tomas So what do you find interesting? What is important for you?

Diana I just live my life, Tomas, I don't have to find it—I don't have to analyse it. If you think what you're doing is important, good for you.

Tomas Not just for me, for everyone. So important, and so simple. Not like politics. Politics they make difficult because it's not really important, they make it all up how it matters. Biology *is* important so they don't have to make it complicated so it's easy.

Diana laughs

Why are you laughing? My English?

Diana Your enthusiasm.

Tomas Yes, I am enthusiasmic. Astic. It's good to be. There is not enough enthusias ... asm. (*He laughs*) You're right, we can't do nothing about the way we are. We don't have to. We are the most marvellous and interesting animal in the world. Only that's not enough for people, they don't want to just be animal, not even the best in the world, they want to be God or something so they make up a big lie about what they are and why they do things and everything gets complicated and nobody's happy. I want to wipe that lie, Diana. This is my ambition. I want to show how when that lie goes it all gets simple.

Diana What does?

Tomas Everything. All of life. How to live. I could show you how beautiful the world is. So complicated, like a cathedral, it loses your breath, but also, Diana, so simple.

Diana I'm not sure I want the world simple, Tomas.

Tomas Why is that?

Diana I don't know what I'd lose in the process.

Tomas Your uncontent you'd lose.

Diana Discontent. (*She stands, holding her glass to her lips, examining Tomas*)

Tomas looks steadily at Diana, then puts his glass down and takes a few steps towards her

Diana (*turning away*) So you knew Josef wouldn't be here.

Tomas I don't think he likes much to be with me. You know he had a big row with my father years ago, before he came here. We had argument about that.

Diana I suppose it's natural to take your father's side.

Tomas In politics, you mean? My father doesn't have a side. He does what he likes to do. He is newspaper editor, he is very good at that.

Diana Good at following the Party line.

Tomas It's not what he wants, he don't want someone else tells him how to do his work for him.

Diana But he does it anyway.

Tomas So what should he do, work in a beer factory? Come to England and be like Josef?

Diana At least Josef can say what he likes, write what he likes, he doesn't have to—

Tomas What you mean? Josef can talk with his old men. He can write what he likes but it don't get published. Is that worth to lose his work, lose his wife? For what?

Diana So you just don't understand why he came over.

Tomas Oh yes. For freedom. The big word freedom.

Diana And that means nothing to you?

Tomas Of course it means. I want freedom. I came to England for freedom: freedom to do my work.

Diana That's not freedom, it's selfishness. Josef didn't come here for himself.

Tomas For who then? For his wife, for Czechoslovakia? Listen, things start to change in Poland and Hungary and Germany, maybe even my country some time, people come on the streets and shout. What you think they shout for, some big abstract? No, they shout for bread for themselves, meat for themselves, freedom for themselves, real freedom, no abstract. I'm a young man, Diana, like you keep saying, I don't start war, I don't push people down, I'm too busy doing what I want to do, yes, being selfish. I don't want to talk against Josef, but if you think he does more good things with his abstract freedom than I do with my selfishness you have to tell me what it is he does.

Diana Is this the kind of thing you say to Josef? No wonder you upset him.

Tomas I say what I think is true. I don't see wrong in that.

Diana Then it's time you did.

Tomas To say truth is wrong now?

Diana Tomas, maybe you don't need to believe in anything, but most people do, their beliefs are part of the property of their lives, they have to be respected like any other property. Don't be so bloody patronizing!

Tomas I can't talk lies, that's all. What you call property of people's lives, is lies! . . . I didn't come here for battle, Diana.

Diana What did you come here for?

Tomas shrugs

Have you eaten?

Tomas I'm OK.

Diana Stop sulking. Do you want something to eat?
Tomas OK. Thank you.

Diana looks at him for a moment

Diana Can you cook?
Tomas No.
Diana Then you can watch. Come on. Talk to me about Prague.

Black-out

SCENE 8

The same. Later the same evening

Diana, a glass of red wine in her hand, sits comfortably on a chair. Tomas sits facing her; he also has a glass of wine. "Der Rosenkavalier" plays on the CD

Tomas No no, you want to have it both ways. I tell you how life comes out of not-life, and you say "Yes, Tomas, I know how we came, I live in the twentieth century, I don't believe in God or miracles." But also you keep those words somewhere in your head, God, miracle, because you like the feeling they give you. You're a hypocrite, Diana.
Diana Yes all right, Tomas.
Tomas No is not all right! Is a lie, is a fairytale! We're grown up now, we say the truth. Billions years ago some bits of molecules got together by luck, by chance, and now we are here, that's enough! We don't need those miracle words, we throw them off our backs, and *then* it gets simple, *then* we make ourselves free, *really* free, free from magic, free to make our chances and make ourselves best we can. Because we live, because we are so lucky to be alive! That's not enough for you? To be free to be alive?
Diana No.
Tomas So what else you want?
Diana I don't know. Something. Nothing you can help me with, Tomas.
Tomas You think I'm too young? I'm very old, Diana, I know everything ... Look, I show you something. Give me your hand.
Diana My dear young man—
Tomas I won't eat you either. Please, Diana, give me your hand. (*He crouches in front of her and holds out his hand*)

Diana gives Tomas her hand, which he holds palm upwards

Diana Are you going to read my future?
Tomas No. Your future you make yourself. The past I read. The making of your hand, out of some bits of molecules, nothing else. No big plan, no God saying, "This is how I want finished hand to be". Just millions of years to adapt, to make it the best. Look at it now, Diana, this perfect thing. (*He holds her hand upright*) Think how it's clever, how it's sensitive, how it can do whatever you tell it, such a marvellous instrument. It comes

out of the sea and the river and the mud, nobody planned it, look at it. Look! It's yours. Your freedom, here is your freedom.

Diana (*after a pause*) May I have my hand back?

Tomas This something else you talk about, what you can feel but you can't define what it is—I think this is like when you have your leg cut off and afterwards you still feel it ache. Only this thing was not cut off because it was never there. What you think is aching never existed. Tell yourself that, and the ache will stop.

Diana (*after a pause*) I think it's time for you to go.

Tomas nods. He stands, but remains looking at Diana

Tomas Nothing comes out of Heaven. Nobody looks at us, nothing happens, only we do it. Us, alone. On our own. This is all it is. (*He is still for a moment, then moves behind Diana's chair. He puts a hand on her shoulder, then the other hand on her other shoulder*)

Diana does not move

Tomas moves his hands to massage Diana's neck gently, then down above her breasts, then to cover her breasts. He is still for some moments

Diana stands up; Tomas's hands fall. Diana turns to look at Tomas; they remain for some time looking at each other

Diana comes round the chair to stand facing Tomas. She undoes the buttons of his shirt, unhurriedly, pulls it out from his belt, draws it aside to expose his chest and belly. She runs her hands once up and down his body then pulls it over his shoulders and stands, her hands on his shoulders, looking at him

Diana Go on then. Make it simple for me.

There is the sound of the front door opening

Tomas turns to look toward the door

Go into the kitchen.

Tomas exits

Diana switches off the CD

There is a knock on the door

Come in, Josef!

Pavlicek enters; he is carrying his hat

Pavlicek Am I disturbing you?
Diana Tomas is here.
Pavlicek Tomas?
Diana He's in the kitchen.
Pavlicek Ah. How nice.
Tomas (*off*) Hallo, Josef!

Tomas comes in

Pavlicek Tomas. This is a pleasant surprise.

They shake hands

Tomas (*to Diana*) I washed the dishes. (*To Josef*) Diana gave me very good supper.

Pavlicek You should have told me you were coming, I'd have come back earlier.

Diana Do you want a drink, Josef?

Pavlicek Thank you, but I think I've had enough for this evening. We became a little maudlin. How are your studies?

Tomas OK, thank you. You are well?

Pavlicek Oh yes, yes yes yes. Top hole. So, what shall we do, have a little party?

Tomas Please, Josef, you must excuse me now. I am just leaving. There is some work I must do. We must meet properly soon.

Pavlicek Yes, we must. Diana has been meaning to invite you. We can have a jolly threesome.

Tomas shakes Pavlicek's hand, then turns to Diana

Tomas It has been nice to talk to you. Thank you for the supper. I hope you will enjoy the book. (*He holds out his hand*)

Diana (*taking his hand*) Goodbye, Tomas.

Tomas goes to the door, opens it, gives a little bow, and leaves

Pavlicek So.

Diana Why did you get maudlin?

Pavlicek Hm? Oh, reminiscing. Somebody said: "I'd give anything to see again a sight I remember from my childhood; a horsedrawn fire engine chasing a fire, bells ringing, four horses at full gallop, the driver whipping them on . . ." Oh, I will have a drink. (*He pours two scotches and hands one to Diana*) Did I hear *Rosenkavalier* as I came in?

Diana Why don't you put your hat down?

Pavlicek I have mixed feelings about Strauss. I don't trust him. Nothing to do with politics. To do with whether he meant it, really meant it. That lovely waltz, for instance—(*He hums a bit of a waltz*) No, not meant it, felt it. Or was he just manipulating us? Does it matter? It works, it's beautiful, it makes you want to cry with delight. Does it matter if it's camp or kitsch or meaningless? It can't be meaningless if I feel it, that's its meaning surely . . . Did you have a nice talk with Tomas?

Diana Oh yes, very pleasant.

Pavlicek What did you talk about?

Diana Oh, reality and abstraction, that kind of thing. How to live . . . He brought me a book to read, that's why he came. He'd promised it.

Pavlicek On how to live?

Diana He thinks if we understand our muddy origins we'll stop being unhappy and dance about.

Pavlicek You must read it quickly. Then perhaps I shall borrow it. You heard what's happening in Hungary? Unbelievable! Whatever next, eh? *Na zdravi! (He drinks)*

Diana Soon perhaps you can go back to Prague.

Pavlicek To do what? Teach Czech?

Diana They'll throw out the party hacks and you can take over.

Pavlicek They'll need young people. Like Tomas. Not old men who jumped ship twenty years ago.

Diana Stop feeling sorry for yourself.

Pavlicek It's the drink.

Diana Then stop drinking.

Pavlicek No no, it improves again later . . . Did you have a chance to read my play?

Diana Yes I did. It's very interesting.

Pavlicek Interesting . . . You think Adrian will like it?

Diana There's rather a lot of politics in it.

Pavlicek It's a political play.

Diana I mean perhaps you could prune it a little.

Pavlicek I've already dropped it in to Bush House.

Diana Ah. Well, we'll see . . .

There is a pause

Pavlicek I really ought to go to bed. (*He stands, as if to go*) Oh I know what I meant to say. A room has become vacant in the house where lives one of my friends. If I want it I'm to let him know quickly. Use of kitchen. I don't want to outstay your kind welcome. (*He pauses*) Yes, I'll take a look at it now. A little cutting perhaps. Who wants politics? All they want to know is if he gets her. Does he get it in, get it over, what does one say . . . ? Goodnight, Diana.

Diana Goodnight . . . Josef!

Pavlicek Yes?

Diana I'm not pushing you out.

Pavlicek You wouldn't, would you? (*He moves to the door*)

Diana Do you want to go to bed?

Pavlicek I'm on my way.

Diana I meant with me.

There is a pause

Pavlicek For me, or for you? . . . I don't need your pity, my dear.

He exits

CURTAIN

ACT II

Scene 1

The same. Evening

Music is playing on the CD player

Diana is sitting with a glass of whisky. Tomas stands behind her, his fingers on her neck

Diana That's how you first touched me.
Tomas I did a good thing, yes?
Diana Oh yes. A very good and brave thing.
Tomas Oh, not so brave. There was not much danger.
Diana How were you to know? What if I'd got on my high horse, Tomas? What if I'd said "How dare you!" and told Adrian his young man was two-timing him, and he'd thrown you out?
Tomas What is two-timing?
Diana Deceiving. Betraying.
Tomas But I knew you wouldn't do something like that.
Diana How did you know?
Tomas Diana! You think I started all this? I said to myself, "Now I'll put my hands on Diana's neck and hope for something"? I tell you truth, I'm a little coward. You wanted my hands on your neck so I put them there. You're clever, Diana. You get what you want and make it look like it was somebody else's idea.
Diana (*with a wry laugh*) Well it's done now, whoever did it. I've got you now, no escape for you.
Tomas And if I try to escape . . . ?
Diana I'll tear you to pieces, my lad.
Tomas Like a tiger?
Diana Tigress.
Tomas Maybe I won't then. (*He kisses the top of her head*) I love you, Diana.
Diana For what that means?
Tomas Come to bed, I show you what it means.
Diana Oh I know. It means a gene wants to make another gene, isn't that right? Only they're flogging a dead horse, aren't they, Tomas, my love? (*She turns off the music, then pauses*) Have you seen Adrian?
Tomas (*sitting*) No.
Diana I had a letter from him. He said he'd seen you.
Tomas Maybe in the canteen in Bush House I said "Hallo" once.
Diana He said you went to his place. He said you had a long talk.

Tomas I told you, I said "Hallo" in the canteen.

Diana He's very angry. He wants you back. He wants me to give you back to him.

Tomas Like property?

Diana Yes.

Tomas And what did you say?

Diana Nothing. He can't have you. You're my property now.

Tomas And if I decide I don't want to belong to anyone like property?

Diana I told you, I'll tear you to pieces ... Why do you want to go to Prague?

Tomas To see what's happening. Just for some days.

Diana I thought you weren't interested in politics.

Tomas This is not politics. This is people trying to get what they want. I want to see that. Anyway I have business.

Diana What sort of business?

Tomas My own business.

Diana It's not that I don't want you to go, my love, it's that I don't want you not to be here. It frightens me. It reminds me of next year when you'll leave me for good.

Tomas We don't think about that. We make what we can now, yes?

Diana Unless I keep you here. You can grow a beard. We'll stage a suicide, leave your jacket on the Embankment with a note. "I cannot leave my love, so I end it here. Tomas Kratky."

Tomas Why is Adrian angry?

Diana Oh, Tomas. You don't know? You used him, didn't you? You took him for what you could get from him, then you found something better and dropped him. A nicer flat, a prettier body.

Tomas Are you meaning this?

Diana Isn't that the way it is?

Tomas I didn't ask him for anything. He wanted to give me things, I said yes instead of no, that's all. He is—himself, he is ...

Diana His own man?

Tomas Yes, his own man. He could make his own choices. Of course I like to live in his flat, if he gives me things I like I take them, what else? If I did wrong, tell me what it was I did. I should not take what he wanted to give me? Or I should stay with him always because he wants me to? I should not be here now? Tell me.

Diana What are you upset about? I'm not blaming you.

Tomas And what about you? You took me from him. You think that was a nice thing to do?

Diana I think it was a lovely thing to do.

Tomas Ah. Maybe there was some revenge there, yes? Because your husband left you.

Diana Maybe.

Tomas You don't care about that?

Diana Why should I? It's what people do.

Tomas And what about Josef? What you did to *him*.

Diana I didn't do anything to him. What are you talking about?

Tomas Diana ...

Diana Have you seen him?

Tomas No, not after that night. He's OK. He's in a nice room, better than he had before. Not much better, but better.

Diana How do you know?

Tomas I heard ... Diana, you are in a mood and I don't understand what it is. What do you want?

Diana Nothing. You. And I've got you. I bought you, I paid a high price for you.

Tomas What price?

Diana Don't you know? And what a fool's bargain! I've only got you on a short let. Next year you'll be off, and what will I have to show for it? Memories? What good are they? So take care, Tomas. I know what the deal is. I know what I've given away. I want my money's worth. So take care.

Tomas Diana, why do you make everything so complicated? I want us to be happy, this is all I know. I want to be with you, I want us to be happy. You want something more from me? I haven't got nothing more ... Please, be happy ...

Diana Yes ... Yes, Tomas ... Yes, my child ... (*She moves to him, laughing. She kneels in front of him, clasps him and pulls him to the floor with her*) Yes, yes, yes, yes. Yes, Tomas, yes! (*She bites him*)

Tomas cries out in pain

Black-out

SCENE 2

The same. Morning

The curtains are still closed. A tray, with the remains of a microwave meal on it, is on the floor. Also evident is a half-empty bottle of whisky, with the top resting nearby

The telephone begins to ring

Diana enters from the bedroom, wearing her nightclothes. She answers the telephone

Diana (*into the telephone*) Hallo ... No I don't want any ... My windows are fine, thank you! (*She puts the phone down, stands for a moment and then opens the curtains. She looks at her watch*) Oh God ... (*She picks up the tray*)

The doorbell rings

Diana puts the tray down on the table and hurries into the bedroom. She re-enters wearing a dressing-gown. She picks up the whisky bottle and screws the top back on, puts the bottle in the drinks cabinet and then exits to the hall

Diana enters with Adrian, who is carrying a holdall

Adrian I hope I haven't got you out of bed.
Diana I overslept. I didn't sleep very well.
Adrian So long as I'm not disturbing anything.
Diana What are you doing here? What's the bag for?
Adrian Not to worry, I'm not moving in. I'm just off to the country for a week. I decided I deserved a break. Get a bit of fishing in, commune with nature and so forth. I thought I'd drop in on the way to sort a few things out.
Diana What things?
Adrian Did I send you a letter?
Diana Yes you did. Don't you know?
Adrian It was the middle of the night, I wasn't sure if I'd dreamt it.
Diana It was foul.
Adrian Yes, well, I was feeling pretty bloody that night and I've no animals to kick in my bijou semi-basement. Domiciles, my love, *habitaments*, that's what I want to talk about. You going to offer me a drink?
Diana Help yourself.
Adrian (*moving to the drinks cabinet and pouring himself a drink*) One for you?
Diana No. You can't stay long, someone's calling.
Adrian Anyone I know?
Diana Pavlicek.
Adrian Oh is he now? So *that's* why you're not dressed!
Diana I told you I overslept!
Adrian I'll cut it short then, for both our sakes. Did you read that play of his?
Diana Yes.
Adrian My God. Why the hell did you let him send it to me?
Diana I told him it was rather political—
Adrian Political? It was bloody terrible! He doesn't have the first idea. But of course you'd have been kind about it, left it to me to tell him.
Diana You weren't rude about it?
Adrian Yes I was, as a matter of fact. Why should I be kind all the time? . . . And I didn't want him sending me a "draft two." Poor old chap. Young Kratky's still abroad, I take it.
Diana Yes.
Adrian Who paid his fare? You, I suppose.
Diana Yes.
Adrian That was kind of you. Worth it, was it? I mean did he come up to expectations?
Diana I didn't have any expectations.
Adrian Did you not? I did. Amply fulfilled I must say, but I only wanted his body. He's a clever lad, isn't he? Though between you and me, I think he actually prefers women, other things being equal. Which they weren't in

this case, I couldn't give him his own room, we had to muck in together. Have you had word from him?

Diana No.

Adrian No. How long's he been gone?

Diana A couple of weeks.

Adrian Well you've had your fun.

Diana What?

Adrian Or are you expecting him back?

Diana Why shouldn't I?

Adrian He won't be exactly *persona grata* with his Czech friends here, will he?

Diana Adrian, I haven't the faintest idea what you're talking about.

Adrian You mean you haven't heard?

Diana Heard *what*?

Adrian No, of course you wouldn't have. Dubsky only told me this morning. I had to nip into Bush House for some scripts I've got to read, no peace for the wicked, he was there of course, Saturday or no Saturday, I think he lives there. He was full of it.

Diana Full of what!

Adrian Apparently young Tomas has been a naughty boy. Sending messages to the enemy. As was.

Diana Sending what?

Adrian Informing, old love. Petty spying, sending reports back, who said what to who, you know the kind of thing.

Diana Reports on whom?

Adrian His compatriots, who else? Do buck up. Are you shocked?

Diana I don't listen to Bush House gossip.

Adrian Ask Pavlicek. It was his lot found out. According to Dubsky he got in a rare state when they told him, he stormed out and hasn't been seen since. Wasn't in his room last night. So, if he turns up you'd better be extra nice to him, as only you know how. Though personally I don't see what the fuss is all about, I thought they *all* did it.

Diana Would you mind going, Adrian?

Adrian Yes, I don't want to be around if he arrives, he can do his crying on *your* shoulder. Not his month is it? You throw him out, I reject his play, his godson's a mole—

Diana What do you mean, threw him out? Who said I threw him out?

Adrian Oh, did you not?

Diana I didn't throw him out. He decided to leave. He found a room. It was always temporary, that was the understanding. Is Dubsky putting it about that I threw him out?

Adrian Oh Di! Come off it, love! Stop playing the little girl, for Christ's sake! It's a real world you live in, not fairyland. Damage can be done. You casually pick up an old chap and take him into your home, you let him shag you on a regular basis and then you say it's temporary. And I'm sure he agreed with you, but what do you think he felt about it? What do you think he hoped about it? . . . Then you take up with his godson, who

happens to be your husband's boyfriend but what the hell, and start
shagging *him*. No hard feelings, Josef, no promises made, out you go.

Diana It wasn't like that at all! You're twisting it round!

Adrian Stating the facts, old thing. And all done in your inimitably passive
way, I'm sure. I lived long enough with you to know how you operate. In
fact all in all I think you've behaved pretty bloody abominably. Do you
think that's fair?

Diana I'd like you to go, Adrian.

Adrian Apart from the French farce aspect. Bush House was full of it for
weeks, as you know ... I've had a word, incidentally, about security; these
various odd bods wandering into the building as of right. Dubsky's due
for an official bollocking. (*He pauses*) You probably never noticed,
Diana, you were too wrapped up in yourself, but in my superficial way
I've always tried to behave moderately morally, by my lights anyway.
Don't shit on your own doorstep, don't poach from friends, that kind of
thing. You remember asking if I was serious? Well I was, as it turned out;
bloody serious. Don't worry, it was all on my side. But at least he was
there ... You hurt me, I was bloody hurt. I cried, Di, long and hard,
many nights. No permanent damage, of course, you know me, no depth,
water off a duck's back. No. He's a very simple lad, you know, a very
simple view of life. In short, totally self-centred, you must get on well
together. He was using me, of course, right, left and centre, I soon twigged
that. You probably have yourself. Not that I minded most of the time, it
quite amused me, made me feel like a doting uncle. He's *like* a child, no
malice in him. Buy him a bag of sweets and he'll take your hand and look
into your eyes and smile and say "Thank you" nicely and it almost seems
like the real thing. Do you find that? (*He finishes his drink at a gulp and
goes to get another*)

Diana Are you driving?

Adrian No. Train ... I really dropped in to talk about the flat. You should
have grabbed at that first offer I made, you know, while you had the
chance. It was a mad idea, I don't know what I was thinking about.
Feeling guilty, I suppose. Anyway, I need the money now, I'm not fond of
semi-basements you can't swing a cat in, let alone human company.

Diana I haven't got any money.

Adrian You'll be getting an official letter.

Diana You mean sell the flat.

Adrian I can't think of anything else, can you?

Diana Will that make you feel better?

Adrian What?

Diana I said will it make you feel better.

Adrian I don't know. I hope so ... So you're not bothered about Kratky's
little games? To tell you the base truth, I was half hoping you'd throw *him*
out as well. If he comes back. I'll have him back if you do, tell him that, no
hard feelings. I'm more pragmatic than you, I'll muck in with anyone.

Diana Push off, Adrian. Fuck off to your fishing, will you.

The telephone rings

God, this is awful . . . (*She goes to the phone*) Hallo! . . . Yes . . . Oh hallo
. . . He's what? . . . What's he done? . . . (*She listens, nodding*)

Adrian picks up his bag

Adrian Have a good weekend.

Adrian leaves

Diana Yes . . . Yes, of course . . . Where is he? . . .

Black-out

SCENE 3

A Hospital Ward. Afternoon

There is a bed, with bedside table

*Pavlicek is in a wheelchair, asleep. One of his legs is in plaster and sticks out in
front of him. A cushion lies on the floor behind the wheelchair*

*Diana enters, carrying a bag of grapes. She stops and looks down at Pavlicek
for a moment*

Diana Josef . . . Josef . . .

Pavlicek grunts

Josef!
Pavlicek What . . . ? Oh it's you. What the devil are you doing here?
Diana I've brought you some grapes.
Pavlicek Who told you I was here? Dubsky, I suppose.
Diana He rang this morning. How are you?
Pavlicek Interfering busybody. I specifically ordered him not to.
Diana Why?
Pavlicek For reasons of my own.
Diana Do you want them washed?
Pavlicek Do I want what washed?
Diana The *grapes.*
Pavlicek Wait a minute. I feel a little confused. I need my cushion.

Diana picks up the fallen cushion and puts it behind his back

Pavlicek That's better.
Diana How are you?
Pavlicek Fine, fine. I like it here, I hope they'll keep me in a long time. It's
like a kind of jolly limbo, all bustle and stasis, time goes on but history has
mercifully stopped. No property needed, even the pyjamas belong to the
State. My only responsibility is not to wet the bed. When they throw me
out I might break the other leg.
Diana How is it?

Pavlicek It's fine. I carry a spare. Where are the grapes?

Diana puts the paper bag of grapes on the bedside table, tearing open the paper to expose them

(*Taking a grape*) Actually Dubsky's been very good to me; telephoned my landlady and so on. He even offered to go and fetch anything I needed, but I couldn't think of anything. He bought me some shaving gear. He's a lonely man, you know. I'd never realized. He stayed here for over an hour today talking about himself. (*He eats a grape*)

Diana What happened?

Pavlicek Didn't he tell you?

Diana He said you fell in the river.

Pavlicek Yes, I happened to be drunk and I slipped. Luckily the river police were passing and heard my cries. I've never been to hospital by boat before.

Diana Where was it?

Pavlicek On the South Bank. *Off* the South Bank.

Diana Outside the Film Theatre?

Pavlicek Why should it be outside the Film Theatre? No, it wasn't outside the Film Theatre.

Diana Where then?

Pavlicek A little along from the Film Theatre. Does it matter where?

Diana There's a railing up all the way along there. A waist-high railing. To stop people falling in.

Pavlicek Well it didn't stop me, did it? It's incredible what drunks can do. (*He reaches across for a grape*)

Diana (*moving the grapes away from Pavlicek*) Josef, will you stop lying to me!

Pavlicek What are you talking about? I've told you what happened, what else do you want?

Diana You couldn't fall in the river there, drunk or sober, without climbing over the railing.

Pavlicek So I must have climbed over the railing, mustn't I?

Diana Why?

Pavlicek Shall we say to sit on it? Shall we say for my own private reasons? And I don't like being called a liar. Anyway it's not your concern is it?

Diana If I'm concerned it's my concern.

Pavlicek And your concern is your own concern. You're English, you wouldn't understand. May I have my grapes back?

Diana Not till you tell me the truth. It can't have been an accident.

Pavlicek I've lived most of my life without grapes, I think I can manage.

There is a pause

Diana gives Pavlicek the grapes and he eats one

I told you, I'd been drinking. I was feeling sorry for myself, and drank some more to stop feeling sorry for myself and felt more sorry for myself and drank some more. .... I looked across the river—to where you *can't* see the Houses of Parliament; it all looked rather beautiful, and I suddenly realized it hadn't the faintest idea I was there ... It's not a sheer wall, you know, the other side of the railing, there's a series of ridges and ledges down to the water. I know it was stupid, I'm too old for it, but drunks can do that kind of thing sometimes. I climbed over the railing, I didn't jump, I mountaineered down and stood on the bottom ledge, with the wall behind me and the black water beneath.

Diana What the hell for?

Pavlicek Because I wanted to! Because there was nobody and nothing there to give a damn anyway so why shouldn't I ... ? Because I wanted to see what it felt like to stand between life and death. I knew you wouldn't understand. I didn't know the water was so shallow, it's too murky to see even in daylight.

Diana So you wanted it to be deep.

Pavlicek Of course I did! What would be the point of standing there otherwise?

Diana And then what?

Pavlicek I must have slipped, mustn't I! And fell, and hit the bottom and broke my leg, which drunks are not supposed to do. Are you satisfied now?

Diana Was it a cry for help?

Pavlicek Oh don't be fatuous! I'm not going to talk about it any more. I don't need your sympathy, I'm perfectly capable of feeling sorry for *myself*.

Diana You're a bloody idiot.

Pavlicek I'm capable of knowing that too. Thank you for coming, supper will be along in a minute, I think it's fish pie. I like fish pie but I don't like being watched eating. And thank you for the grapes. How much were they, I'll pay you for them.

Diana I didn't try to hurt you, Josef.

Pavlicek Oh do stop it!

Diana What?

Pavlicek It doesn't need pleas for the defence, my dear. This isn't nineteen sixty-eight, it's nineteen eighty-nine. Your Prague Spring is over and done with.

Diana I don't know what you're talking about.

Pavlicek It's a grimy world full of grimy betrayals! One gets what one can! You think *Tomas* tried to hurt anyone? He got caught, that's the only difference! Stop being so damned romantic!

Diana Why are you being so beastly to me?

Pavlicek Because I love you, why do you think? And I want to be shot of it ... Europe boils over, Czechoslovakia enters a sort of Spring, Pavlicek confesses his November love. Good for a short story. It doesn't matter, none of it matters ... I'll tell you what I *really* remember about falling in the river; leaning drunkenly against that railing, thinking, "This is like the Titanic going down." The film, you know. Bulkheads buckling, everything sliding and sloping together. Thinking, "What does it matter that I can't write plays, that I'm a failed journalist, that I've got no country, that my room smells of cabbage, that I betrayed Tomas? What does it matter to Czechoslovakia what happens to me?" Then I thought, "What the hell

does it matter to me what happens to Czechoslovakia?" Bump, slop. Then
I'd *like* to say I clambered down to the ledge above the dark water to try
to work out if the world would miss me; or if I would miss the world, one
of the two. If it mattered, if any of it mattered . . . Only I don't remember.
I only remember sitting in the mud with a broken leg. Covered in sick.

Diana What do you mean, betrayed Tomas?

Pavlicek Nothing.

Diana Why has everything got so dirty? . . . Is there anything you want?

Pavlicek No. Everything's laid on here.

Diana Do you need any money?

Pavlicek Are we back to that again? We don't need money here, Diana.
This is the last enclave of the socialist paradise. I was a socialist, you
know, once upon a time.

Diana You want to buy newspapers and things.

Pavlicek Dubsky looks after me. (*He looks off*) Oh look, the trolley's
arriving!

Diana (*getting up*) I'll call in tomorrow.

Pavlicek Dubsky's coming tomorrow.

Diana That doesn't stop me coming, does it?

Pavlicek Do I have to be brutally frank? I don't want you here. You disturb
me, I don't want to be disturbed . . . You want my advice? Get what you
can. That's what it's all about. Transactions. Well transact . . . Oh, you'll
find out soon enough, you may as well know now.

Diana Know what?

Pavlicek It was my idea.

Diana What was?

Pavlicek I was hurt and I wanted to see you hurt. Moderately despicable,
not uncommon . . . I persuaded my friends we should do something about
Tomas. We all put on our best suits and trotted off to the Czechoslovak
Embassy. They said they'd see what could be done. They said they'd talk
to the Home Office. They want to be on the right side . . .

Diana Why did you do it?

Pavlicek Because I felt like it! . . . The prognostication is hopeful.

Diana (*after a pause*) You stupid old man.

Diana exits

Black-out

SCENE 4

Diana's flat. Night

Music is playing on the CD player

*Diana is standing by the window, looking out, a glass in her hand. After a
moment, she leaves the window, picks up the whisky bottle, considers for a
moment and then refills her glass*

The front door is heard to close, off

Diana puts her glass down and switches off the music

Tomas enters, carrying a holdall. He wears an unbuttoned coat over his other clothes

Tomas Hallo.
Diana (*very quietly*) Hallo, Tomas. What took you so long?
Tomas There was some trouble on Piccadilly Line, somebody said a bomb-scare. But I am here now.
Diana So you are.

Tomas puts the holdall down. He goes to Diana and takes her hands

Tomas (*concerned*) You are glad to see me again?
Diana Oh Tomas. (*She embraces him*) Oh my lovely boy ...
Tomas That means yes?
Diana It's just as if somebody pulled a switch. An engine starts to purr. Can you feel it? I am required again, Tomas, by the blind gods. My lovely, lovely boy.
Tomas Diana, have you been drinking a lot of whisky?
Diana Yes, I'm afraid I have. You shouldn't have taken so long getting here. Did you have a good time in Prague? Is it still beautiful?
Tomas Yes of course. Listen, I was on BBC TV. I was in Wenceslas Square in the big demo, BBC camera pointed to me so I waved, did you see it?
Diana What were you doing there?
Tomas I wanted to go and look, it was very exciting, you should be there, you should have been there ... Diana ... Oh I bought, brought you something. Bought and brought. Some weeks in Prague and my English loses. (*He opens the holdall and takes out a cardboard box*) You want to open it?

Diana opens the box and takes out an item wrapped in newspaper. Unwrapping it, she finds a small glass ornament

Be careful, it breaks. This is not from a souvenir shop, this is old glass. I don't tell you what I spent for it. You like it?
Diana It's beautiful.
Tomas I got a little thing for Josef too. How is he, did you see him?
Diana He's broken his heart.
Tomas He what?
Diana He broke his leg.
Tomas Josef? How did he do that?
Diana In the river. He fell in the river.
Tomas (*laughing, then stopping guiltily*) No, I don't laugh. Was he drunk?
Diana Yes.
Tomas Silly man. I shall visit him. Is he in hospital?
Diana He doesn't want to see you.
Tomas Why not? He'll like me to talk about Prague.
Diana He doesn't want to see anyone. Only Dubsky. Dubsky looks after him.

Tomas Is there something wrong, Diana?

Diana Oh something is wrong, yes, something is dreadfully wrong. And it's all your fault, you stupid boy. I told you to take care, didn't I?

Tomas What are you talking about, what is it that happened?

Diana Oh ... I'll tell you later.

Tomas Why you don't tell me now?

Diana shakes her head

You are mysterious, Diana. (*He takes her in his arms*) You know, all the journey I was thinking, soon I will be with Diana. Then the train stopped in between the stations and people looked, you know as if they wanted to be dead or something, and I thought: I don't mind. Soon I will be with Diana. And here I am, and here you are, beautiful like always ...

Diana What a pretty speech ...

Tomas I mean it, I mean it!

Diana I know you do, my love, my love ...

Tomas And did you miss me a little bit?

Diana Oh yes. I died, I kind of died. But then I decided you weren't coming back.

Tomas What are you talking about? Of course you know I come back! Listen, I tried to telephone, but they couldn't get a—a *line*, and then I was going to send you a letter, only—

Diana Sh-sh-sh. Stop it, stop it. No more talking.

Tomas Listen, Diana, shall we go to bed now?

Diana To swear eternal love?

Tomas To make nice things together.

Diana Oh yes. Oh yes ... Only we can't, not yet.

Tomas Why not?

Diana Somebody's coming.

Tomas You invited somebody?

Diana He called earlier. I said you'd be back. He has to see you personally.

Tomas Who?

Diana looks at him for a moment without speaking

Diana My God, you are so young ... Oh my God ... Go and put your things away.

Tomas Diana—

Diana Do as I say.

Tomas hesitates, uncertain. Then he picks up his holdall and exits to the hall

Diana picks up her present to look at it

There is the sound of a police siren from outside

Diana switches on the music again

   Tomas returns

Tomas What did you do in my room?

Diana doesn't answer

My things are all over, it looks like a mad animal was in there. And my papers are gone ... I can't talk with that music.

Diana turns the music off

Tomas Diana, I ask a question.

Diana I was looking for something.

Tomas You have to break things to look for something?

Diana There are your papers.

Tomas Ah.

Diana It took me ages to read them, my Czech is rusty and your handwriting is dreadful. Did you make fair copies? Did you type them out neatly?

Tomas I suppose Josef told you about it, I can imagine how he told you. My father had a stupid letter from him, he showed me, it was—I don't know the word.

Diana Vile?

Tomas Vile, yes.

Diana What did your father say about it?

Tomas About the letter?

Diana About what you'd done.

Tomas But he knew already. I asked him at the first, what do you think?

Diana And he said do it?

Tomas Listen, if I said no, they don't give me visa, they don't give me money, I can't come to England, I can't do my work. He said "Go ahead of course, if that's what you've got to do then do it, why not, everybody does it, it's like a game."

Diana Is that how you thought of it?

Tomas Yes, a silly game, what else, who cares about it?

Diana Josef cared.

Tomas Oh, Josef! What hurt did I do to him? He thinks someone comes over with a poisoned umbrella for his old men? Diana, they are like old tigers in a zoo with no teeth, nobody gives a damn about them. If I did something to hurt them, you tell me what I did!

Diana You betrayed them, Tomas.

Tomas What you mean, betrayed? I don't use words like that.

Diana You don't think it means anything? To betray somebody?

Tomas OK, you want to use this word, you better use it on Josef. Himself he betrayed, long ago, himself as a man. His life has been a betrayment of himself. He doesn't like to live in the real world so he puts on a funny hat and plays being a funny foreigner and turns himself into a joke person. Don't blame me for that!

Diana And me, do I live in the real world?

Tomas What are you talking about?

Diana You wrote about me too.

Tomas What will I write about you?

Diana Don't lie to me, Tomas. I know you, I've read you, you're there, I've read you through. (*She gestures to the papers*)

Tomas OK, I tell them I talk to some World Service people. Why not, it looks good for me and what difference does it make? You think they bring bomb over for Bush House now? They are fools, I play a game with them. You can read what I wrote.

Diana I have. Drama as a cultural weapon.

Tomas Yes, silly stuff like that.

Diana Do you remember where I was when I talked that silly stuff?

Tomas How would I remember?

Diana I was in bed. We were in bed. We were playing one of our games, don't you remember? To keep talking? I had to keep talking while you did things to me. Do you remember what you were doing while I talked about drama as a cultural weapon? And I lost, didn't I, I stopped, I cried out, "Oh God, no I can't, Oh God, I'm dying . . ." Something like that.

Tomas I didn't remember that.

Diana Then some grubby bureaucrat in some grubby office read it over, copied it down—

Tomas So what? They don't know about that!

Diana *I* know about it!

Tomas So what? . . . Diana, we are talking about nothing! . . . Listen, if I did something you don't like I'm very sorry. But look at me, I am here now, I am the same person you like to be with. Nothing has happened, no blood, no bombs. We are so lucky to be here together, to have some time to use together. Listen—Diana, I am a bit tired after the journey, and you are a bit drunk, yes? Just a little bit? So that we talk rubbish. So let's go to bed, shall we do that? No more talking, like you said.

Diana Just tell each other we love each other?

Tomas Yes, why not?

Diana Say silly stuff to each other? Like "I love you, Diana." And I know what it means when you say that, it means you're coming. "I love you, Tomas, Oh God I love you for ever, this goes on forever!" And that means I'm coming. And the genes smile, don't they, they don't know, do they? . . . Only we can't, I told you, not yet.

Tomas Who is this who's coming?

Diana A policeman. Someone from the Home Office. I don't know how it works.

Tomas What do they want?

Diana They'll give you a bit of paper I expect. To say you're undesirable. That's what they call it.

Tomas What are you talking about?

Diana They're sending you back, don't you understand? I'm surprised they let you come back, bureaucracy I suppose, or maybe they like giving you the bit of paper.

Tomas But why, why?

Diana Josef fixed it, Josef and his old men. If you hurt someone they hurt you back. They did something at last. They struck a blow for Czechoslovakia.

Tomas To send me back? They can do that? For that little thing I did?

Diana They all want to be on the right side, you see, the Czech Embassy, the Foreign Office. You're on the wrong side now, you're undesirable.

Tomas I don't believe this . . . Didn't you do nothing about it?

Diana What could I do?

Tomas You could tell Josef not to do this! You could tell him you kill him if he does this! You could ring somebody, you could see somebody! Did you do any of this?

Diana No.

Tomas Why not?

Diana I think if he hadn't done it perhaps I would.

Tomas Diana, I don't know what you are saying.

Diana You've dirtied everything up, Tomas. You've soiled the bed, you stupid child.

Tomas You would send me away? You don't love me now?

Diana Of course I bloody well love you. I wish to hell I didn't. I'm sick with love for you and I want it to stop, I want it to leave me alone! I don't want to want you! Oh my love . . . (*She takes him in her arms for a moment, then releases him*) I thought I'd seen the last of you. I thought you weren't coming back. I went into your room, I read all your stuff, all your secrets, I turned your room over like a policeman. Looking for something, I don't know what. Some—message, something that said it meant something, it wasn't just another muddy coupling, it wasn't just two bodies writhing together. You made me a promise, do you remember? You were going to make it simple for me, make life simple. Well you have, haven't you! You're going away and what are you leaving?!

Tomas What do you want I leave you? I don't know what anything of this is about. We both know from the start I have to go away some time. You seem to blame me for it. What do you want that I give you? Tell me what it is, if I have it I give it to you!

Diana Tell me you love me, Tomas. Tell me our love was made in heaven and will last forever. Tell me you can't live without me, tell me you'll never forget me. Tell me it meant something!

Tomas What you want it to mean?

Diana shakes her head dumbly

What do you want from me? That I lie about things, you want me to lie?

Diana Yes! Why not? That's what we do! Why not!

Tomas Because I don't lie like that! I give you what I have to give you! I love you while I am here! This is all I can do because this is all it is! You want love made in heaven you have to go somewhere else! You want to lie you must find someone else to lie with, I will not lie with you! Why you spoil it now, why you spoil our last times! You think this is love, what you do now? You think to break my room up because you can't have me for ever is love? Love is to be together and make the best with the time! Not to waste it like this . . . You can't have me for ever so you want to tear me to pieces. I tell you I love you, I often say that. You say, "What do you mean?" I say I mean I want to be with you and want to be in bed with you, which is all I know it can mean. But that's not enough for you, you want some abstract love when I'm not here. I don't think anything I give you will be enough for you. You want the future, I can't give you that, I only

know about what happens now ... You see this? (*He picks up the glass ornament*) I take two days to find this, to find the best. This is not from souvenir shop, Diana, this is real old glass. Somebody took a lot of trouble to make this, then a lot of people keep it safe for a hundred years or so. Here ... (*He gives it to her*) It will break some time. You might as well break it now. Take it, break it. Then it's done. (*He goes to the door*)
Diana What shall I write in my diary? "Tomas Kratky was here? We loved one another? He left me a piece of Bohemian glass?"

Tomas exits

Diana looks at the ornament. Still holding it, she pours herself another drink. She turns on the radio. A talk programme is heard. Diana switches the radio off. She puts on the CD player. "Der Rosenkavalier" is heard. Diana finishes her drink and pours another. She begins to cry, softly at first, then louder, more extravagantly, like a frustrated child

The doorbell rings

Black-out

SCENE 5

The café area of the departure lounge at London Airport. 1992

The scene begins with Tomas and Diana in their positions from Act 1 Scene 1

Tomas You are going on holiday? Can I buy you a coffee or something else?
Diana I've got something coming. (*She gives a sudden quick glance, towards the bar, then back to Tomas*)
Tomas Ah.
Diana What were you doing here?
Tomas I told you, business. I'm a business man now, you see. (*He indicates his clothing*)

Diana looks at him seriously

Tomas gives a little deprecatory laugh

Diana So you're not going to write books and become famous?
Tomas Aha. I remember that. I was a young man then.
Diana Three years ago.
Tomas Three years can be a long time. A lot of things have happened to me, I'm a grown-up man now. I have a little boy, you know. Another Tomas. He looks like me.
Diana And a wife?

Tomas Yes, a wife too.

There is a slight pause

Diana They've called your flight.
Tomas That's OK. (*He sits looking at her, smiling slightly*) So how are you, what are you doing now?
Diana I'm in advertising; making commercials. I mean I work for a company that makes commercials.
Tomas Good money?
Diana Yes, quite good money.
Tomas And you are happy?
Diana Oh yes. And you?
Tomas I'm busy. Whenever I'm busy I'm happy. .... You are beautiful as always.

Diana looks at him for a moment

Did I say something wrong?
Diana No no.
Tomas Listen, you must come to Prague, see how it is now. I will show you around. You can stay at our house. We have a big house.
Diana Thank you.
Tomas I think about you sometimes. You think about me sometimes?
Diana Yes, sometimes.
Tomas We had good times then.
Diana Yes.

There is a pause. Tomas sits smiling at Diana

What happened?
Tomas Happened?
Diana When you got back?
Tomas Oh, you mean that silly business. That was OK. My father took care of that.
Diana Your father? How?
Tomas Well you know how they have an official committee now to look at who did what thing in those times. To find who is pure. (*He gives a little laugh*) More silly politics, you see. Anyway, my father helps on that committee.
Diana So you're pure.
Tomas (*laughing*) Yes, I am pure. Not that it matters to me. I mind my *own* business ... Ah! Listen, Diana, I've got something for you. (*He picks up his case*) Do you remember the piece of glass I gave you? You still got it, did it break yet?
Diana No, I've still got it.
Tomas That's what I make now, genuine Bohemian glass, very good stuff. We have a good little factory, my father and I, ten workers, more next year we hope. I tell you, so many chances in Czechoslovakia. Everything is to start. You wait a few years. We don't come with our hat for help

then, you see. Maybe you come to us. (*He laughs, opens his case and brings out a cardboard box. He gives the box to Diana*)

Diana opens the box and takes out a piece of glass rather like the one she has already

My present for you.

Diana Thank you. (*She puts the ornament back in its box*)

There is a last call for the Prague flight

Tomas So, I must go. (*He stands, looks at her for a moment*) Come to Prague, I give you a good time. Goodbye, Diana.

Tomas exits

Adrian enters carrying two glasses of whisky

Diana I said coffee.

Adrian I thought you might need this instead.

Diana Oh, you saw him. You should have come over. We could have had a jolly reunion.

Adrian Do I see a glistening tear of the eye? You're not going to cry, are you? Pecker up, old chum. Things come and things go . . .

Diana Don't be so bloody trite.

Adrian And the jolly old world keeps turning, my romantic darling.

Diana You're a bastard, Adrian.

Adrian That's my girl. You can cry tonight. We'll get pissed and cry on each other's shoulders, shall we do that?

Diana He's a business man. He's selling genuine Bohemian glass.

Adrian Smart suit. What's this, a free sample?

Diana We can put it on the mantelpiece with the other one.

Adrian takes the glass ornament out of the box

You see? It's just as good if you don't go too close. And if you break it you can buy a replacement. He's got a child.

Adrian Who's a clever boy then? Did you tell him we're each other's lodgers again?

Diana No.

Adrian Why should you? Keep your options open.

Diana I didn't *not tell* him. I just didn't tell him.

Adrian Absolutely.

There is a slight pause

Diana There was a young fellow from Prague . . . Whose habits . . .

The call goes out for the Lisbon flight

Adrian Gate eight. We shall exit on a rhyme.

But they take time to finish their drinks

There's a lot to be said for the duck . . . Apart from the rhyming with fuck

... It bobs on the surface and never gets wet ... (*He goes from poetry to prose*) Pops its beak down into the muck now and then, snuffles about, finds something tasty, pops up again bright as a pin, and you'd never know.

Diana (*finishing her drink and standing*) Come on, old pal. (*She picks up a bag*)

Adrian picks up the rest of the bags. His eyes meet Diana's over the cardboard box

Diana exits

Adrian follows her

CURTAIN

FURNITURE AND PROPERTY LIST

ACT I

SCENE 1

The café area of the departure lounge of London Airport

On stage: Table
Chairs
Diana's hand luggage
Bag of duty-free goods

Off stage: Executive briefcase **(Tomas)**

Personal: **Diana:** newspaper

SCENE 2

The Living-Room of Diana's Flat

On stage: Sofa
Dining table
Chairs
Drinks cabinet *In it:* bottles, glasses
CD player
Radio
Telephone
Pile of papers

Off stage: Thick foolscap envelope **(Adrian)**
Mug of cocoa **(Diana)**

SCENE 3

On stage: As Act 1 Scene 2

Re-set: Whisky bottle and glass

Set: **Pavlicek**'s hat

Strike: Pile of papers
Foolscap envelope

Off stage: Tray *On it:* coffee pot, cups, saucers, milk jug, sugar bowl **(Diana)**

Personal: **Pavlicek:** wristwatch (used throughout play)

On stage: As ACT I Scene 2 without pile of papers

Re-set: Whisky bottle
Glass

Set: Word processor components
Cardboard boxes
Diana's handbag. *In it:* purse *In it:* ten pound note

Strike: Tray and contents

Off stage: Black exercise book **(Diana)**
Glass of water **(Diana)**

Scene 5

The South Bank of the Thames

On stage: Bench

Personal: **Pavlicek:** hat

Scene 6

The Club Room at Bush House

On stage: Table
Two chairs

Off stage: Tray. *On it:* two cups of tea
Walking sticks **(Adrian)**
Briefcase. *In it:* papers **(Adrian)**

Scene 7

The Living-Room of Diana's Flat

On stage: As Act 1 Scene 2 without pile of papers

Off stage: Book **(Tomas)**

Personal: **Diana:** Papers (from Scene 6), handbag. *In it:* Compact disc of *Der Rosenkavalier*

Scene 8

On stage: As Act 1 Scene 2 without pile of papers

Re-set: Whisky bottle
Glass

Set: Two glasses of red wine

Strike: Book
Papers

Personal: **Pavlicek:** hat

ACT II

SCENE 1

On stage: As Act 1 Scene 2 without pile of papers
Set: Glass of whisky for **Diana**
Strike: Wine glasses

SCENE 2

On stage: As Act 1 Scene 2 without pile of papers
Set: Tray. *On it:* remains of microwave meal, cutlery etc.
          Half-empty bottle of whisky
          Whisky bottle top

SCENE 3

A Hospital Ward

On stage: Bed
          Bedside table
          Wheelchair
          Cushion

Off stage: Bag of grapes **(Diana)**

SCENE 4

The Living-Room of Diana's Flat

On stage: As Act 1 Scene 2 without pile of papers

Off stage: Whisky glass **(Diana)**
          Holdall. *In it:* Cardboard box. *In it:* Small glass ornament wrapped in
          newspaper

SCENE 5

The café area of the departure lounge of London Airport

On stage: Table
          Chairs
          Diana's hand luggage
          Bag of duty-free goods

Off stage: Executive briefcase containing cardboard box.

In it: Small glass ornament wrapped in newspaper **(Tomas)**
          Two glasses of Whisky **(Adrian)**

Personal: **Diana:** newspaper

LIGHTING PLOT

Practical fittings required: nil

Various interior and exterior settings

ACT I, Scene 1

To open: General lighting

Cue 1   **Diana:** "Yes." **Tomas** sits smiling at her   (Page 2)
         Black-out

ACT I, Scene 2

To open: General lighting

Cue 2   **Diana** exits   (Page 5)
         Black-out

ACT I, Scene 3

To open: General lighting

Cue 3   **Pavlicek:** "Good."   (Page 10)
         Black-out

ACT 1, Scene 4

To open: General lighting

Cue 4   **Diana:** "There's a warden down there."   (Page 14)
         Black-out

ACT 1, Scene 5

To open: General lighting

Cue 5   **Diana:** "Let's celebrate."   (Page 18)
         Black-out

ACT 1, Scene 6

To open General lighting

Cue 6   **Diana** ruffles **Adrian**'s hair   (Page 21)
         Black-out

ACT 1, SCENE 7

To open: General lighting

Cue 7   **Diana:** "Talk to me about Prague."   (Page 25)
           Black-out

ACT 1, SCENE 8

To open: General lighting

Cue 8   **Pavlicek** exits   (Page 28)
           Black-out

ACT II, SCENE 1

To open General lighting

Cue 9   **Tomas** cries out in pain   (Page 31)
           Black-out

ACT II, SCENE 1

To open: General lighting

Cue 10   **Diana:** "Where is he?"   (Page 35)
           Black-out

ACT II, SCENE 3

To open: General lighting

Cue 11   **Diana** exits   (Page 38)
           Black-out

ACT II, SCENE 4

To open: General lighting

Cue 12   The doorbell rings   (Page 44)
           Black-out

ACT II, SCENE 5

To open: General lighting

EFFECTS PLOT

ACT I

Cue 1   When the CURTAIN rises   (Page 1)
           General hum of airport noises; the departure of a flight to Prague
             is announced

Cue 2   **Diana** "Yes." **Tomas** sits smiling at her   (Page 2)
           Fade airport noises

Cue 3   As ACT 1 SCENE 2 begins   (Page 2)
           Music plays from the CD player

Cue 4   **Diana** sips her coffee: **Pavlicek** watches her   (Page 5)
           Sound of a police car passing

Cue 5   **Diana** switches on the radio   (Page 21)
           World Service news report is heard

Cue 6   **Diana** switches CD player on   (Page 21)
           "Der Rosenkavalier" is heard

Cue 7   **Diana** exits into the kitchen   (Page 21)
           Doorbell

ACT II

Cue 8   As ACT II SCENE 1 begins   (Page 29)
           Music plays from the CD player

Cue 9   As ACT II SCENE 2 begins   (Page 31)
           Telephone rings

Cue 10   **Diana** picks up the tray   (Page 31)
           Doorbell rings

Cue 11   **Diana:** "Fuck off to your fishing, will you?"   (Page 34)
           Telephone rings

Cue 12   As ACT II SCENE 4 begins   (Page 38)
           Music plays from the CD player

Cue 13   **Diana** looks at the ornament   (Page 40)
           Police siren

Cue 14   **Diana** switches on the CD player   (Page 40)
           Music plays

Cue 15   **Diana** switches off the music   (Page 41)
           Cut music

Cue 16	**Diana** turns on the radio *Talk programme is heard*	(Page 44)
Cue 17	**Diana** turns the radio off *Cut radio*	(Page 44)
Cue 18	**Diana** puts on the CD player *"Der Rosenkavalier" is heard*	(Page 44)
Cue 19	**Diana** starts to cry *Doorbell*	(Page 44)
Cue 20	As ACT II SCENE 5 begins *General hum of airport noises*	(Page 44)
Cue 21	**Diana:** "Thank you" *The departure of the flight to Prague is announced*	(Page 46)
Cue 22	**Adrian:** "There was a young fellow from Prague ... Whose habits ..." *The departure of a flight to Lisbon is announced*	(Page 46)

MADE AND PRINTED IN GREAT BRITAIN BY
LATIMER TREND & COMPANY LTD PLYMOUTH

MADE IN ENGLAND